Manifesting with Awareness

Manifesting with Awareness

21 Days to Create from Intention and Presence

Translated from the original Spanish edition:
*Manifestar con conciencia: 21 días para crear desde la intención y
la presencia*

Elvira Sombra

ISBN: 979-8-9956492-4-3
Published by Sombra Editorial
First English Edition: 2026
Printed in the United States of America

Dedication

To those who are in the middle of a process
and still choose not to give up.

To those who feel the desire to change their lives
and have made the conscious decision
to look inward with honesty.

This book is for those who allow themselves
to imagine the person they are becoming
understanding that real change does not come from
urgency, but from an inner commitment to their own
transformation.

May these pages walk beside you as you choose to
grow, heal, and create a life that feels more aligned
with who you truly are.

Table of contents

Introduction

A Conscious Pause to Return to Yourself

This is not a book for those seeking quick answers or formulas that promise immediate results.

It is an invitation for those willing to look at themselves honestly and take an active role in the creation of their own life.

This space was created as a conscious pause.

Not to escape the world but to return to it with greater clarity.

To slow down.

To listen.

To observe from where your decisions, your desires, and your expectations are being created.

We are used to moving forward without questioning. To desiring without examining where that desire comes from.

To manifesting without realizing that, even unconsciously, we are already creating.

This book begins with a simple yet powerful truth:

You don't begin manifesting when you ask for
something new.

You are already manifesting all the time.

The difference lies in whether you are doing it
from reaction… or from awareness.

This is not about becoming someone else.

It is about recognizing who you are when you quiet the
noise around you and allow yourself to be present with
honesty.

You will not find perfect answers here.
You will not find promises of certainty.

You will find questions.
Practices.
Pauses.

Spaces designed to help you take responsibility
for what you are choosing to create.

Manifesting, in this context, is not about controlling life.

It is about learning to relate to it from a place that is more present, more aligned… more true.

If you choose to continue, do so with openness.

Not to demand results but to allow yourself a process.

CHAPTER I

Manifesting with Awareness

Understanding the Process Before Walking It

Manifesting is not magic. It is not constant positive thinking, nor repeating empty words while waiting for life to respond.

It is not denying pain, rushing your process, or forcing yourself to "stay high vibration" when inside you feel exhausted.

Manifesting with awareness is not about appearing well or maintaining an optimistic version of yourself when something hurts.

It is not a way to avoid discomfort or bypass the inner work that is asking for your attention.

Awareness does not promise comfort.
It invites honesty.

Manifesting is a conscious process that requires
presence, clarity, and active participation in your
emotional, mental, and practical life.

It does not happen only in the mind, nor is it limited to
what you wish to attract.

It is built through the way you think, feel, decide, and
act each day even when you are not aware of it.

You are already manifesting, even unconsciously.

Your decisions, your reactions, your silence, your
patterns they all create.

Understanding this is not meant to blame you.
It is meant to return your responsibility… and your
power.

Not everything that happens in your life is your
responsibility.

But how you choose to respond to it… is.

Taking responsibility does not mean carrying the past
or demanding perfection from yourself.

It means recognizing that you have a real margin of
participation
in what you choose to sustain today.

And from that place, reclaiming your ability to create
with greater awareness.

Manifesting with awareness invites you to look deeper.

Where is your desire coming from?

- From expansion… or from lack?
- From a genuine longing… or from an unhealed wound?
- From growth… or from the need for validation?

Not all intentions come from the same place.

And recognizing that changes everything.

The same desire can come from escape… or from choice.

From fear… or from clarity.

The difference is not in what you want but in the place within you from which you name it.

Manifesting is not about controlling outcomes or
forcing timelines.

It is not about reacting only to what happens outside of
you.

It is about learning to direct your attention toward
what you are choosing to create aligning intention,
emotion, word, and action while accepting that there
will be moments of clarity and moments of resistance.

Both are part of the process.

Sometimes resistance is not an obstacle.
It is a signal.

An invitation to listen to the part of you that needs
attention before moving forward.

Awareness does not eliminate doubt.
It teaches you how to relate to it… without running
away.

Imagine, for example, the desire for a career change.

It is not only about the position you want
or the outcome you imagine.

It is about where that desire is coming from:

Are you trying to escape exhaustion?
Or to build something that truly supports you?

Are you seeking external recognition?
Or a deeper internal balance?

Conscious manifestation begins when you ask these
questions not when you send the application.

The Five Essential Steps of Manifestation

A conscious structure, not a rigid formula

The steps you are about to explore are not rules.
They are not guarantees.

They do not promise immediate results or perfect
outcomes.

They are a structure a way to observe how you
participate, consciously or unconsciously,
in the creation of your everyday life.

This is not about following instructions.

It is about using these steps as a mirror a framework
for self-awareness.

A way to recognize:

1. what you are holding onto
2. what you are avoiding
3. where your choices are coming from

To explore them, we will use a simple and familiar
example:
the desire for a more aligned work or life stage.

Step One: Clear Intention

Naming with honesty

You cannot sustain an intention that has not been named truthfully.

Clarity does not come from vague phrases or undefined desires.

Saying,
"I want to feel better"

is not the same as saying:
"I desire stability, peace, and an environment where I can grow without feeling constantly on edge."

Naming a clear intention also means letting go of other possibilities.

Every time you choose honestly, something else is left behind.

And that can create discomfort.
Even fear.

That is why we often stay in vague desires because they do not require commitment.

9

Before writing your intention, ask yourself:

1. What am I truly seeking?
2. What part of me needs this?
3. What would change in me if this became real?

Clarity does not require certainty.
But it does require emotional honesty.

Exercise
Write your intention as honestly as possible:

____

____

____

Step Two: Aligned Emotion

Feeling before seeing

Manifestation is not only about thinking.
It is about allowing yourself to feel.

Emotion is the bridge between intention and action.

But it is also a mirror.

Sometimes it reflects calm, excitement, or expansion.

Other times, it reveals fear, doubt, or resistance.

All of it matters.

If discomfort appears when you imagine your desire
observe it.

Do not rush to fix it.

Emotion carries information that needs to be heard
before you move forward.

Alignment does not mean feeling good all the time.
It means being honest about what is present.

Reflection

When you imagine your desire:

What emotion appears first?

____

____

____

Where do you feel it in your body?

____

____

____

Step Three: Words and Thought

Your inner dialogue as direction

The way you speak to yourself either supports or sabotages your process.

This is not about replacing negative thoughts with forced positivity.

It is about choosing language that is honest and compassionate.

There is a difference between: "This never works for me"

and

"I am learning to hold something different from what I've known."

Words do not create magic. But they do create direction.

Your internal dialogue influences:

1. the decisions you make
2. the way you interpret your experiences
3. and how you move forward

The language you choose may not define the outcome but it does shape the path.

Exercise

When you think about your desire:

What phrase appears most often in your mind?

____

____

____

Does it support you or limit you?

____

____

____

Now, gently reframe it from a more honest and compassionate place:

Instead of:

____

____

____

You could say:

____

____

____

This is not about convincing yourself of something you don't feel. It is about speaking to yourself in a way that does not abandon you in the process.

Step Four: Aligned Action

Moving even without certainty

Manifesting is not waiting for perfect signs.
It is taking small, real actions aligned with your
intention even when fear or doubt is still present.

Alignment does not require big, immediate change. It
requires consistent, honest steps.

Sometimes, a small action repeated over time creates
more transformation than an intense but inconsistent
effort.

Movement itself is part of manifestation.

Exercise

What is one small, real action you can take in the next
few days?

____

____

What fear or resistance appears when you think about
taking that step?

____

____

Even with that fear, what is one commitment you can
make to yourself?

____

____

This is not about doing more. It is about moving
without betraying yourself.

Step Five: Trust and Surrender

Letting go of control

Trust is not the absence of action. It is the release of control.

After doing your part, learning to let go becomes an act of emotional maturity.

Not because you don't care but because you recognize that not everything depends on you.

Trust, in this context, is not passivity.

It is inner rest.

Reflection

What part of this process are you trying to control too tightly?

____

____

What would it look like to release some of that control without abandoning yourself?

____

____

Write a phrase that reminds you, you have already done your part:

____

____

Trust is not forgetting your intention. It is allowing life to participate in it.

CHAPTER II

The Process in Practice

Gratitude, Alignment, and Conscious Action

This chapter does not introduce new concepts.
It asks something more demanding: to live what you
already understand.

Understanding a process is not the same as
experiencing it.

Many ideas can feel clear in your mind… and still not
transform your life.

Practice is where awareness stops being a concept and
begins to become a way of living.

This is not about doing things perfectly. It is not about
following a ritual.

It is about observing, in your daily life, where your
decisions, your words, and your actions are coming
from.

Practice is not meant to produce immediate results. It is
meant to create internal coherence.

Manifesting in practice is not a single act or a specific moment.

It is a way of relating to yourself while you choose, doubt, move forward, and pause.

It is learning to stay present even when there is no certainty.

Move through this chapter without rushing.

Not to correct yourself but to become aware of what is already happening within you.

Gratitude as a Starting Point

Recognizing Before Asking

Before asking life for something new, pause and recognize what is already supporting you.

Not as a requirement.
Not as a technique.

But as an act of presence.

Gratitude does not exist to deny what is missing.
It exists to reorganize your perspective.

When you practice gratitude with awareness, your attention shifts.

You stop focusing only on what is lacking and begin to see the fullness of your experience.

Not because everything is resolved, but because you choose to see your life as a whole:

1. what hurts
2. what is missing
3. what remains

Gratitude does not mean settling.

It does not mean giving up what you desire.

It means recognizing where you are starting from.

Gratitude does not replace desire.
It grounds it.

Reflection

Before continuing, ask yourself honestly:

1. From where am I desiring something new?
2. From urgency, exhaustion, or comparison?
3. Or from a conscious and grounded choice?

Take a slow breath…

Allow your body to settle before writing.

Gratitude Exercise

Acknowledge what you can appreciate today, even if it is not perfect.

Today, I am grateful for…

____

____

____

Thank you.
Thank you.
Thank you.

STEP ONE: NAMING YOUR INTENTION

Clarity as an act of responsibility

A clear intention gives direction to your process.

Not as pressure but as responsibility toward yourself.
Naming your desire honestly means recognizing what you truly need in this stage of your life.

Not what you think you should want.
Not what others expect from you.

Not all intentions come from the same place.
Some are born from growth and expansion.
Others from exhaustion, fear, or unhealed wounds.

None are wrong.

But all deserve to be observed with awareness.

Naming your intention also requires commitment.

When you choose clearly, you let go of ambiguity. And ambiguity often feels safer because it does not ask you to move.

Before writing your intention, pause:

1. What am I truly seeking right now?
2. What part of me needs this?
3. What would change within me if this became real?

Clarity does not require certainty.
But it does require emotional honesty.

Exercise · Your Clear Intention

Take a breath before writing.
Do not look for the "right" intention.
Look for the most honest one.

My clear intention is:

____

____

____

STEP TWO: FEELING BEFORE SEEING

Emotion as information

Emotion is not a requirement to attract something. It is information about how you relate to your desire.

Allow yourself to feel what it would be like to live what you are creating.

Do not imagine ideal results.

Notice real sensations.

Do you feel:

- calm
- excitement
- resistance
- fear
- doubt

Everything that appears is valid.

Aligned emotion is not always comfortable. Sometimes it reveals parts of you that need attention before moving forward.

Ignoring that information does not accelerate your process it only makes it more confusing.

Feeling before seeing does not mean forcing yourself to feel differently. It means allowing yourself to listen to what is already present.

Exercise · Emotional Awareness

If this desire were already real, today I would feel:

____

____

____

When I imagine it, the strongest emotion that appears is:

____

____

____

What might this emotion be asking me to notice before I move forward?

____

____

____

STEP THREE: THE POWER OF WORDS

Your inner dialogue as direction

The way you speak to yourself directly influences the way you move through your process.

Your words do not create magic but they do create direction.

This is not about lying to yourself or repeating positive phrases that do not feel true.

It is about choosing a language that supports you instead of punishing you.

Especially when:

- you doubt
- you make mistakes
- things do not go as expected

Your internal dialogue has a real impact on your energy, your motivation, and your decisions.

Before trying to change your thoughts, observe them.

How do you speak to yourself when things don't go as planned?

Exercise · Inner Dialogue Awareness

Before (a phrase I often repeat):

____

____

____

Now (a more honest and compassionate version):

____

____

____

This is not about forcing positivity.

It is about choosing words that do not abandon you while you grow.

STEP FOUR: TAKING REAL STEPS

Action as alignment

Manifesting is not waiting until you feel ready.

It is moving with honesty even when there is still fear or uncertainty.

Aligned action does not need to be big.

It needs to be real.

A small step, sustained over time, creates more transformation than an intense effort without consistency.

Sometimes action is not about doing more.

It is about doing differently:

- choosing better
- setting boundaries
- asking for help
- organizing your priorities

Before taking action, pause and ask yourself: Does this honor my intention or is it just trying to calm my anxiety?

Exercise · Conscious Action

This week, my aligned action will be:

____

____

____

If fear or resistance appears, observe it but do not stop. Moving with respect for yourself is also a form of manifestation.

STEP FIVE: TRUST AND SURRENDER

Faith as inner rest

Trust is not the absence of action.

It is the release of control.

After doing your part, letting go becomes an act of emotional maturity.

Not because you do not care but because you understand that not everything depends on you.

Letting go does not mean disconnecting from your desire.
It means releasing tension around it.

Allowing life to participate.
Trust, in this context, is not passive.

It is inner rest.

Exercise · Conscious Surrender

Take a slow breath before writing.

What part of this process have I been trying to control too tightly?

____

____

____

What would it look like to release some of that control while still caring for myself?

____

____

____

Write a phrase that reminds you, you have already done your part:

____

____

____

Trust is not forgetting your intention.
It is allowing life to meet you there.

CHAPTER III
Integration

From Intention to Everyday Life

Manifestation is not integrated when you understand a concept.

It becomes real when you begin to live from that understanding even on the days when you don't feel clear, aligned, or motivated.

Integration is not about maintaining an ideal state.

It is about learning to return to yourself again and again even when you get distracted, when you doubt, when you feel tired.

Awareness is not proven on the easy days.

It reveals itself in the way you choose to relate to yourself when the process becomes ordinary.

This chapter is not meant to transform your life in twenty-one days.

It is not about reaching a final destination.

Its purpose is more real than that:
To help you live what you have learned while you choose, doubt, move forward, and pause.

Manifesting is not about doing it perfectly.

It is about returning to yourself every time you lose your way even just a little.

The practices in this chapter are not a challenge.
They are not a demand.

They are an invitation.

If one day you don't write, you have not failed.
If one day you doubt, you have not gone backward.

Awareness does not break with pause.

It strengthens when you choose to return without judgment.

Daily Manifestation Practices

21 Days to Integrate the Process

These practices are divided into three weeks.

Each one serves a different purpose, but all of them support one another:

Week I: Presence and Gratitude

Week II: Clarity and Alignment

Week III: Action and Trust

Do not rush ahead.

Integration happens when you respect your own timing.

WEEK I
PRESENCE AND GRATITUDE

34

Slowing down before creating

This first week is not designed to "activate" anything. It is designed to deactivate the automatic patterns from which we often try to manifest.

Without presence, desire becomes escape.

Without gratitude, intention comes from lack.

This is not about being grateful to receive something. It is about recognizing where you are starting from.

Gratitude does not require you to feel good. It invites you to see more clearly.

Day 1
Recognizing What Already Supports You

Take three slow breaths.

Let your body settle before writing.

Ask yourself: What in my life has supported me even when I didn't notice it?

Write three simple things you can be grateful for today.

They can be small:

1. A place to rest
2. Someone who listened
3. Your body continuing, even on difficult days
4. A routine that gives you structure
5. Simply being here today

The simple things sustain you.

1. _______________________________
2. _______________________________
3. _______________________________

Day 2
Living in Your Body with Kindness

Observe your body without judgment.

Do not try to fix it.

Acknowledge one part of yourself that supported you today even if you usually criticize it.

It could be:

- Your hands
- Your legs
- Your breath
- Your voice

Your body does not need perfection.
It needs presence.

Day 3
Learning from the Past Without Becoming It

Think of a difficult experience.

Not to relive the pain but to extract awareness.

Ask gently:
What did I learn from myself that still supports me today?

____

____

____

The past does not define you.

But it can teach you how to hold yourself better now.

Day 4
Valuing the Ordinary

Appreciate something you usually take for granted.

A moment.

A routine.

A quiet presence.

The ordinary creates stability. And stability is the real foundation of any conscious process.

Notes:

Day 5
Gratitude Without Expectation

Think of someone who has touched your life.

Express gratitude without expecting anything in return.

Not recognition.
Not continuation.

Just acknowledgment.

Gratitude without expectation is a deep form of release.

Notes:

Day 6
Appreciating the Day as It Was

Before sleeping, acknowledge your day without editing it.

Even if it was:

- ordinary
- tiring
- confusing
- quiet

Recognizing it as it was is a form of peace.

Notes:

Day 7
Integrating Without Pressure

Look back on your week.

Do not add anything.
Do not remove anything.

Just observe:
What shifted in me this week?

____

____

____

You don't need to conclude anything.
Just notice.

WEEK II
CLARITY AND ALIGNMENT

43

Observing before moving forward

This week is not about doing more. It is about seeing clearly from where you are creating. Clarity does not always feel comfortable. Sometimes it brings truth before it brings relief.
Both are necessary.

Day 8
Naming Your True Intention

Write a clear intention for this stage of your life:

____

____

____

Then ask: Is this coming from love... or fear?

____

____

____

Observe it honestly.

Day 9
Feeling Your Intention in Your Body

Close your eyes for a moment.

Do not imagine outcomes.

Feel.

What emotion appears when you think about your
intention?

____

____

____

There is no "correct" emotion.

Let it exist.

Day 10
Observing Your Inner Dialogue
45

Notice a limiting thought that repeats throughout your day.

____

____

____

Do not fight it.

Naming it is already awareness.

Notes:

Day 11
Transforming Without Denying

Rewrite that thought from a place of truth not forced positivity.

Before:

____

____

____

Now:

____

____

____

Honesty supports you more than pressure.

Day 12
Choosing a Real Action

Write one small, real action that honors your intention.

____

____

____

Do not choose the ideal.

Choose the possible.

Notes:

Day 13
Acting Without Measuring Results

Take that action.

Do not evaluate the outcome.

Recognize that you moved.

Moving with awareness is already part of the process.

Notes:

Day 14

Recognizing Inner Change

What changed in me by acting with more awareness?

____

____

____

Even if nothing external changed.

WEEK III
ACTION AND TRUST

Sustaining without controlling

This week does not ask you to do more. It asks you to trust differently.

Trust is not giving up.
It is releasing rigidity.

Day 15
Facing What You've Been Avoiding

Do something you've been postponing.

Not perfectly.

Just consciously.

Notes:

Day 16
Resting Without Guilt

52

Allow yourself to rest.

Without explaining.

Without earning it.

Rest does not delay your process.

It supports it.

Notes:

Day 17
Recognizing Your Courage

53

Write about a decision you made without guarantees.

____

____

____

See the courage in you even if you doubted.

Day 18
Letting Go of Control

54

What are you trying to control right now?

____

____

____

Practice releasing it even for a few hours.

Day 19
Appreciating the Process

55

Acknowledge your consistency.

Your honesty.
Your presence.

Even if it wasn't perfect you showed up.

Notes:

Day 20
Honoring Who You Are Now

Write a short letter to yourself.

Recognize:

- what has changed
- what you no longer tolerate
- how you now treat yourself

Notes:

Day 21
Closing with Presence

Take a deep breath.
Repeat silently:

I trust.
I am supported.
I do not need to rush what I am learning to live.

This is not an ending.
It is a conscious pause.

Manifestation does not end here.

It continues every time you choose:
presence over urgency
awareness over pressure
honesty over fear

Each time you return to yourself you are already manifesting.

VISION BOARD

Giving Visible Form to Your Intention

A vision board is not just a collage.

It is not a decorative exercise, nor a list of desires
disguised as images.

It is a conscious integration tool a way of giving visible
form to everything you have been working internally.

After moving through gratitude, clarity, emotion,
words, action, and trust, the vision board becomes a
meeting point between your inner world and your
everyday life.

Not to force results.
Not to convince life.

But to remind you of the direction you are choosing to
live from especially on ordinary days:

when motivation fades,
when your mind becomes distracted,
when routine takes over.

A vision board created with awareness does not try to control outcomes.

It does not demand manifestation.

It works as a symbolic mirror reflecting who you are choosing to become while you create the life you desire.

And like any mirror, it is not there to pressure you. It is there to help you see more clearly.

A vision board is not only about what you want to have.

It is about how you choose to be with yourself while you are building it.

Before beginning, it is important to understand:

The vision board itself has no power.

The power lies in:

- the awareness with which you create it
- and the decisions you sustain afterward

The Real Purpose of a Vision Board

The purpose of this practice is not to visualize in order to obtain.

It is to visualize in order to align.

To align:

- your intention
- your emotions
- your words
- your actions

in a language that your mind and your body can remember even on days when doubt, fatigue, or routine appear.

A conscious vision board:

1. Does not come from comparison
2. Does not respond to external expectations
3. Does not demand timelines
4. Does not promise immediate results

It comes from inner listening.

Before You Create

Preparing your inner space

Before cutting, pasting, or selecting images, pause.

Take a slow breath.

Allow your body to settle.

Return to your main intention.

Focus on how you want to feel not only on what you want to achieve.

When an intention comes from the body, not just the mind, it becomes clearer… and more sustainable.

Ask yourself honestly:

What do I need to integrate in this stage of my life?
What inner quality do I want to strengthen?
What way of living am I choosing to sustain?

Do not look for perfect answers.
Look for resonance.

If something feels forced, it is not ready yet.

If something feels simple but true, it is enough.

Sometimes what transforms you most is not a big goal
but a clear internal direction:

peace

stability

freedom

presence

boundaries

self-worth

rest

What to Include in Your Vision Board

Symbols before goals

A conscious vision board is not built only with external goals.

It is built with symbols that represent internal states, sustained decisions, and ways of living.

You can include:

- Images that represent calm, expansion, or stability
- Words that evoke values, not pressure
- Colors that bring you clarity or grounding
- Symbols connected to experiences you want to live

Not everything needs to be literal.

Sometimes an image does not represent something you want to "achieve" but something you want to feel:

security

lightness

belonging

self-love

You can also include reminders of how you want to
move through the process, not just the result.

For example:

- an image that reminds you to pause

- a symbol of simplicity or order

- a word that represents healthy boundaries

- a scene that evokes rest

Trust what draws your attention.

Your body recognizes before your mind understands.

If something expands you, calms you, or brings clarity
it is already serving its purpose.

Organizing Your Vision Board

Flexible structure, not rigid rules

Some people prefer to divide their board into areas:

- well-being
- work
- relationships
- personal growth

Others prefer a free and intuitive layout.

Both are valid.

What matters is not visual perfection but internal coherence. If, when you look at your board, you feel calm, clarity, or expansion you are on the right path.

You do not need a "perfect" starting point.

Begin with what feels most alive in you.

Sometimes the center of your board is not a goal but a word, a value, or an emotion.

You may choose a central word to guide your board:

presence
clarity
stability
worthiness
calm
trust
freedom

Not to limit you but to bring unity to your energy.

Color and Aesthetic

Feeling before perfection

Color does not manifest anything by itself. The intention behind it does.

Do not look for perfect combinations or external references.

Choose tones that make you feel:

- supported
- grounded
- focused

Your board does not need to look beautiful to others.

It needs to feel true to you.

In this context, beauty is not decoration.

It is inner harmony.

During the Creation

Listening more than thinking

As you place each element, pause.

Ask yourself:

- Does this represent how I want to feel?
- Does this align with who I am choosing to become?
- Am I creating from calm… or from urgency?

If something does not resonate, remove it without guilt.

Letting go is also part of manifestation.

Do not force the process.

If you feel overwhelmed, stop.

Pause is also part of creating with awareness.

You can build your board in stages:

Today you choose images.
Another day you organize them.
Another day you place them.

A conscious board is not created in a rush.

After You Create

Relationship, not control

Place your vision board somewhere visible.

Not to monitor it.
Not to demand results.

But to allow your mind and your body to gently remember the direction you are choosing.

You do not need to look at it every day.

Sometimes a single glance is enough to realign you.

Your vision board is not a contract with life.

It is a conversation with yourself.

It is a compass not to control the path, but to return to yourself when you feel lost.

On difficult days, it can remind you: "This is how I want to live," even if the result is not yet visible.

Evolution and Letting Go

When releasing is also growth

Your vision board can change.

You can update it.
Adjust it.
Or even let it go.

Manifestation is not about holding on to an image.

It is about allowing your process to evolve.

If something no longer resonates, trust that.

Changing your intention is not failure.

It is deeper listening.

Life changes.
You change.
Your vision can change too.

That is not inconsistency.

That is growth.

LETTER FROM THE AUTHOR

If you've made it this far, I want to thank you deeply. Reading this book was not an automatic act. It was a conscious choice.

You chose to pause.
To look inward.
To create space for yourself
to live with more awareness.

This book was not written from a place of certainty. I wrote it while walking my own path.

While learning.
While questioning.
While observing myself in real time.

This is not a book born from theory. It was built through experience through trying, adjusting, and beginning again.

Through learning how to listen to myself. To question my patterns. To relate to my thoughts, my emotions, and my actions with greater awareness.

This book was never meant to give you definitive answers. It was never meant to promise immediate results. It was written to remind you of something essential:

You are already participating in the creation of your life even when you are not fully aware of it.

Manifesting is not about controlling the path.

It is about learning how to walk it with more honesty, more responsibility, and more openness.

Throughout these pages, I invited you to pause.

To recognize what already exists.
To name your intention.
To feel it.
To observe your words.
To take aligned action.
To trust.

Not as rigid steps but as a living practice.
One that you can adapt to your rhythm, your process, your life.

There will be days when you feel clear and aligned.

And there will be days when you doubt.

Both are part of the path.

Manifesting is not about always feeling balanced.

It is about learning to return to yourself every time you lose your way even just a little.

If something in this book resonated with you, trust that.

You do not need to apply everything.
You do not need to do it perfectly.

Sometimes one reflection is enough to begin a deep shift.

Sometimes a conscious pause can transform more than many rushed actions.

I want to leave you with this gentle reminder:

You are not behind.
You are not broken.

You do not need to become someone else to create a life
that feels aligned with you.

You are already in process.

And that… is enough.

Thank you for allowing yourself this space.
Thank you for choosing yourself.

With presence and care,
Elvira Sombra

ABOUT THE AUTHOR

Elvira Sombra is a writer and creator of conscious spaces.

Her work is rooted in a personal journey to understand how we move through everyday life and how presence and inner honesty can transform the way we choose and create.

Through reflective writing and mindful observation, she invites others to pause, to listen to themselves, and to return to what is essential.

Her approach is human, accessible, and grounded free from rigid formulas or promises of immediate transformation.

In addition to her work as an author, she is a wedding officiant, guiding individuals and couples through meaningful ceremonies that honor presence, intention, and conscious choice as acts of transformation.

Her work is an invitation to return to yourself.

www.ingramcontent.com/pod-product-compliance
Lightning Source LLC
Chambersburg PA
CBHW051133160726
47997CB00019B/2357